Yes Poetry

Poetry is the evidence of life;
if your life is burning well,
poetry is the ash.

Leonard Cohen

Yes Poetry

edited by Ruth Hudgens and Michael Smith

SILVERTON POETRY ASSOCIATION · 2007

Book design by John Labovitz, using Adobe InDesign. The typeface is Andulka, by Frantisek Storm of Prague. The book was printed by Heron Graphics on Classic Crest Writing paper, then perfectbound by hand.

The cover image is composed of 100,000 random characters from a selection of the poems in this book. The shape of the tree was generated using an iterative fractal algorithm.

Silverton Poetry Association, 303 Coolidge Street, Silverton, OR 97381
spa@silvertonpoetry.org   www.silvertonpoetry.org

ISBN 978-0-9794736-0-90

Published by FAST BOOKS, P.O. Box 1268, Silverton, OR 97381

WELCOME to this bounty of poems by way of Silverton, a small town in Oregon's Willamette Valley, where poetry is flourishing beyond reason. We asked for poems from all the poets who have read at the Silverton Poetry Festival, a week-long annual event since 2001, or at the monthly open readings sponsored by the Silverton Poetry Association. The response was thrilling in its variety and depth.

Almost all the poets live in Oregon. Strawberries, apples, roses, tomatoes, even eggplant are juicily evoked. Native fauna appear as well, and the seasons, but there are not as many nature poems as one might expect. More of these poems are tales of ordinary experience, mined for meaning or relished in its immediacy. There are poems of memory and the passing of time, of love, death, and war, poems of consciousness and identity, but surprisingly few poems of place. These poets respond to where they find themselves but their imaginations carry them far and wide, unlimited.

Art, perhaps poetry most of all, is the clearest window into each other's inner being. Poetry can be whatever you want, can say anything in any form it chooses to take, and these poets take full advantage of its range. Their individual voices bring us into the heart of the present and open up worlds we have no other way to know.

Ruth Hudgens
Michael Smith

By Association

My parents and grandparents,
and so in my ancestry—

they never took part in
the Silverton Poetry Festival,

and as a matter of fact,
they never even got to Silverton.

Ah, but through my affiliation,
they're part of the Association,

and the sharing is international.

Lawson Fusao Inada

Judith Barrington

Walking North

for Nancy

Think of your life as a beach—
a wide, smooth-sanded Oregon beach
with the sea on your left as you walk north
and on your right a range of dunes
changing outlines from year to year.

Sometimes the sand gleams with mica;
waves slip up leaving a scalloped border
where you tread softly with bare feet.
Sometimes days come crashing in on you,
spittle from the surf flying in your face,
your boots leaving a trail of small ponds.

But always as you head for the mist-hung
headland you will reach one day—always
there's that single set of footprints ahead.
You recognize those prints: your mother made them
long ago when she walked through the years
you've come to know—thirty-five, forty-eight:
always stepping in the faint shadows of her feet.

And then they're gone. Sand stretches away
unmarked except by wind and gulls' feet:
you are as old as your mother was when she took

her final step. For a moment you wonder can you go on?
Icy wind snatches at your scarf and you stagger,
your footprints weaving among a thousand small shells.

Think of your life as a beach you can walk alone
even when mist comes down and you know you are lost.
Walking north, the cold may burn your cheeks.
But when you rest, dunes will hold you on their breasts
and two boys will be walking in the prints you left behind.

Harvest

When you're young and out at night
searching for your lost pony
the black sky leans on your shoulders
like a rucksack full of sins.

Under invisible stars
you carry the burdens: gates left unlatched;
temper-tantrums that sent the pony
bucking away in his field

and all those times
you laughed at the farmer,
a dour man who watched the sky
as harvest approached—

watched the corn ripen while you
and your pony cut the corners
of those brittle fields, flattening
his bread and butter.

When you're young and out at night
calling for your black pony
through field after field of grain,
an owl flings itself down from an oak

and you make vows.
If you only could find the pony
but remember too the vows
you make and remake on a dark night, searching.

Eleanor Berry

Like Anemones from the Blood of Adonis

Heal-all, *Prunella vulgaris*—common
on every continent, this cross of Eurasian
and North American subspecies—especially here
this year when a spring unseasonably cool and wet
followed a winter breaking records for warm and dry.
Now, in early summer, the brush is thick with purple bloom.

Heal-all, self-heal—always and everywhere
needed—ointment from the leaves
to dress torn flesh, tea from the whole plant
to drink for the heart. Greatly needed
now, when no continent is safe from harm.
But the recipes have been forgotten, if they ever worked.

Heal-all, common prunella—royal purple
for the common people—if not a salve or tonic,
then a purple sign of sorrow for the slaughtered
on every continent, so many handsome and young
as the bold hunter beloved of Venus.
Heal-all—springing up everywhere, as if from their blood.

Where Gravity Has Brought Them

Jutting out of the ground, its thin gravelly soil,
the rocks are the bones of the land,
its ribs showing, hips and elbows protruding.

Kicked loose by the hoofs of the cows as they lurch
heavily down the slopes, the rocks are great eggs
this land, once riverbed, lays and lays.

As firs drop cone grenades on roof, deck, lawn,
as maples launch fleets of twirling propellers,
and shining flotillas sail up from thistle heads,

as blackberry canes sag with clusters of swollen
purple globules—with the same wild excess, rocks
tumble down the slopes, into heaps against tree-trunks,

into piles along the sides of steep cow-paths,
roll singly out across the flat pasture below.
There they are, like unforeseen troubles, old sorrows,

undeniable hard objects we stumble on, sometimes fall.
But, when we heft them, they fit our grasp,
worn to hand-sized roundness by the ancient river,

and, when we leave them where gravity
has brought them, they startle us with beauty,
dark gray against the ash gold of dry summer grass.

Karen Braucher

City of Clouds

I thought I was going
to a claustrophobia-inducing
shack, but instead
here I am in a playwright's
spacious writing studio
in Silverton, Oregon,
where he has hung
plywood clouds
from the ceiling.
I don't ask him why.

I'm getting the tour
as a visiting poet.
They're way up high
so we don't hit our heads on
wooden facsimiles of
water hanging in the air.

We're in this tiny outbuilding
of his and his wife's retirement farm,
terrific people with contemporary art
all over their sprawling ranch
and chestnut-colored horses
lounging in a huge stable.
A gigantic window looks out on a field.
There is a Buddha statue
on the path toward the studio
and also—surprise—

a full-length mirror on the porch
across from the entrance/exit.
Don't we writers try to hold it up?

I love this fake city of clouds.
It reminds me
the space
above my head
can be filled with
any damn thing
I want.

Jellyfish

To carry such 3D squiggles
half-baked or crazed
notions   streaming
calligraphy   time-lapse
neon streaks

To expand   a parachute
sink slowly
to the ocean floor   rise
upward   opening
and closing
my crazy umbrella   my filmy
mushroom cap

To swirl   galaxies
in deep space
seen through a telescope
a love that keeps spiraling

To pulse slowly my odd
frills   my oneiric membranes

suspended

like smoke   without bones
translucent   inside a glow

To ascend   dust
off the desert
seemingly innocent
a feminine

rocket
lavishly shedding larvae

To sting
explode on contact
this *medusa*   with
breathtaking poison
paralyzes
your intricately obvious
way of seeing

Instructions

Among hands, be the cat's cradle,
among keepsakes, the one-of-a-kind,
among footsteps, the syncopated soft shoes,
among scissors, the one that scallops.

Among questions, be the unanswerable,
between twins, the sixth sense,
among pairs, the lost glove,
among colors, the autumn rose.

Among weapons, be a disarming strategy,
among doors, the one that opens to thin air,
among the shadows you find on the floor,
be the one that flutters.

Laton Carter

Evensong

Afterward, even our toes interlocked,
her nose whistles. Is she,
she is asleep, and I study the skin around her eyes.

I have wrecked so many of my hours with worry
when the opposite could be true—not
always there, abiding, tolerant with me, but at least

here now:
good possibility.

Stupid and meaningful,
what memory would mistakenly revise later as pivotal,
the calmest of tendernesses,

easily let go as she wakes, pauses,
one eyelid raising—

Like a barrel.
Then a gesture downward,
the back of her thumb tapping the hollow of the belly.

My cooper she smiles, and taps again the drum.

November

In the darkness, I can see your open mouth.
I decide not to wake you,

lift your arm slung haphazardly over my chest
as precisely as I can,
place it between us.

Blood travels back, the nerves unwork their paralysis:
my arm, rushing back to me.

Months after I quit,
Jimmy Dean Rich would call, drunk, from Bakersfield.

He'd been digging ditches,
hated it, it was hot, but it was better I should know.

It was always late and who was this.

I never asked, and the answer would arrive
soon anyway, the same slide pulled up for viewing:

six-foot-five, in a busser's smock like me,
no medication, the epileptic seizures falling him,
curling him up in the dishroom.

Patience

Where the wall meets the ceiling
there in the darkness of the corner,
in a country she can hardly imagine,

there is one just like her,
a girl who likes yellow right now,

a man lonely enough he talks to goldfish.

Hearing his voice against the glass
was like a woman in another country
hearing hers against the practice room wall she sings intervals.

Simultaneousness could mean not chance
but hope. A less than variable connection.

So much of the earth's renderings never to be seen or imagined.

She does,
imagines each night before sleeping,

concentrates her will into that space above her,
the people her age, older, people she wouldn't meet,

one second of a voice exactly her own.

Virginia Corrie-Cozart

Friday Night Jam

The guitar player wears logger pants and suspenders.
He nods the tempo, and five
other music makers start together;
jaws concentrate.
Folks join the circle with mandolins, banjos,
fiddles, lots of fiddles,
and one saxophone.
They gather at the old schoolhouse,
park dusty pickups,
family sedans under the alder trees.
Their heads are full of tunes,
old-timey two-steps, country waltzes,
echoes from the Tennessee hills
and an Illinois play-party
clear out here to Oregon.
The piano man chords an honest progression;
a fiddler with the rhythm in her wrist
goes along the line.
Neighbors come to tap toes, bob heads,
break for coffee and store cookies
laid out on a paper plate, a little gossip.
Players leave, return when they know the piece.
Kids chase. It's easy.
One guitarist goes modern with Les Paul.
A mandolin picker calls for "Planxty Irwin."
The saxophonist (played a 14-year gig
with the v.f.w.) drowns out everyone
on "Bonaparte's Retreat." Nobody minds.
A Bach minuet sounds for a while,
then "Alexander's Ragtime Band" and a long reel.

"Take it home" for one more chorus.
They stop as one, rock back,
 grin at the scattered applause.

We step outside into summer twilight,
 the smell of drying hay,
"Shady Grove" faint behind us.
In the space of a play yard we've meshed
with a hundred years of living or dying.

Far above our heads
the nighthawk careens and cries.

The Dark Ages, 2004

The day after elections
fog, like loathing,
constant as a dull headache,
turned people invisible.
It decayed our valley's
blameless bounty,
shrouded us with fear
that smelled of sulfur
and stuffed a sock
down our throats.

Walt Curtis

Strawberries

I swoon at the flavor
of first fruit—fresh strawberries.
They're from the earth. Oh my God!—
there's nothing like the taste
of Oregon berries picked in the patch.
Sweeter than candy, sort of like fine
wine, but not spoiled by alcohol.
Crimson jewels from the rainy wet
dirt. My heart beats faster—
recalling sore knees, bent back,
muddy blue jeans—berry splotches
dotting my once-white t-shirt—
the sport of strawberry-picking
as a teenager near Oregon City.
We kids hated it, complained
about getting up at 5 a.m.
to board a retired school bus.
Arriving at some farmer's field
way out in Clackamas County.
The dew-wet, cold raspy rows
of green leaves waiting
to be fondled, caressed, combed
by nimble fingers for elusive
fruit jewels. Always June was damp,
misty; gray clouds rained down
mildewing and rotting the berries
unless the sun would come out to play.
Then sunburned face and neck that day.
At lunch maybe a peanut butter and
jelly sandwich, can of pop—eyeing
the girls and avoiding going back

to work in the miserable muddy fields.
Still I would kneel on the ground,
bend my back to pay homage to that time—
to taste again startled sugar,
nectar of the gods. Simply
twiddle off the green stem, and
plop ripe berry ecstatically
in my teenage mouth. What pleasure!
The exquisite form of strawberry—
I dare not delineate it!—
is heart-shaped, pitted,
arrowhead of silken fruit.
Every variety has a different
texture and fragrance: Marshall,
Shuksan, Brandywine, Hood,
Crescent, Michael's Early, Gandy,
Climax, Lovett, Aroma. I savor
the names of strawberries
as they roll from off my tongue.

Flowering Toward Death

The old transparent apple tree down
in the orchard, overrun with blackberry
brambles and deer trails. The white
apples bruise easily, yet so abundant
raining fruit, rotting on the ground,
a carpet of brown and white apples.
Each dry summer stalk of grass stabs
apple flesh, each thud turns that side
of pale apple brown. The deer gnaw away
and the ants at what could have been
apple sauce or green pies, so soft
the fruit there is no shelf life,
a rare variety of pomology. I tell
myself I must clone or graft a fresh
start from the 80-year-old tree, as
it breaks apart producing boxes and
bushels of splendid produce. The limbs
bend, then break—yes, I mean break
with the weight of a glad abundance.
I use boards to prop up failing limbs,
cull and discard green fruit before
rain and sun swell and ripen these
odd apples, delicate tasting and
unforgettable in flavor. Using
plumbing strap and nails I try to
bind the old tree from splitting apart,
shattering its ancient sagging limbs.
My God, what a lesson for old age
and we complaining humans. The
tree minds not at all that it gives its all
before death, is more fruitful than

any season before. It pours its
cornucopia, branches bent and bowed
by a glorious harvest. These last
crops come straight from the heart
and soul of Apple Heaven shouting
out loud with the woodpeckers and
the creak and sag of gnarled limbs.
More fruit before I die! More to
give to the world before I go back
into ground, back into mulch, back
to where I came from. Seed of proclivity,
soil of creativity. The Earth itself,
mother of everything living, proclaims:
The tree of being, the world tree,
never stops giving shining fragrant fruit.

Madeline DeFrees

Climbing the Sky Bridge stair
on my way to Suzzalo Library,

                     I pause on the landing to admire
the *Dancer with the Flat Hat* by Sculptor
Philip Levine. The cast bronze figure enacts his
favorite theme—the ambiguity of
balance—including his own. Work with cement and
metal is brutal. Witness two artificial
knees, a back subjected to the knife and uncounted
injuries to the hands. I tip my head
back to look up at

                     the six-and-one-half-foot
figure, feel positional vertigo
return, and grip the railing to keep from
falling at the Dancer's feet. Given the weight of
the artist's materials, the incredible
feeling of lightness
means a triumph of art over matter. How better
to salvage one's grief
as body slowly turns

                   stone, already tied to
a drowning spirit, than by putting a flat
hat on one's sorrow, making
the soul and its body dance in ambiguous balance?

The Poetry of Swans

October twilit water under the wild swans at Coole
Mirrors a still sky. Against all evidence
a former world believed
swans sing their sweetest when about to die
and on that premise, called its greatest poets
swans: Homer, Swan of Meander,
Virgil, of Mantua, and Shakespeare, Swan of Avon.

Merrill's Black Swan *has learned to enter/Sorrow's*
lost secret center, and the Black Swan
Jarrell encounters on the lake after milking
opens a red beak: inside…darkness…stars and
the moon. The waterbirds settle down
on a pond with reeds and sedge, each to ponder
its own image

              in the black reflective waters where
the rushes grow. *No swan…so fine* as Marianne's
chintz china one with…toothed gold collar on
to show whose bird it was. In the mind's
eye, the watcher sees a mixed flotilla of legendary
swans glide shoreward over silver
waves to animate the shallows, while far away

on still St. Mary's Lake, let Wordsworth's solitary
swan *Float double, swan and shadow.* A shot rings out.
From a height, one whistling swan
falls, crippled, to the water. His departure
song—melodious, soft-muted—a better way to die,
uniting myth and truth in a vain
struggle to rejoin companions in the sky.

The Spider in *Brewer's Dictionary*

Opened, the book released a small
spider: pale, near-sighted,
anonymous. No doubt a scholar of
phrase and fable, who preferred
investigating the shadows. Under
the kitchen's public light, the spider
flinched in the sudden
fluorescence. The meaning I wrenched
from this brief encounter: *Sweetest*
to die doing the work you love best.

Efraín M. Diaz-Horna

A Book

A book
A new path
    An avalanche
A river
A torrent of fresh water
        A mover of rocks.

A book
An avenue
    A rush
An ocean
A fountain of many waters
        A forger of continents.

A book
A seed
    An avatar
A cloud
An accumulation of living kisses
        A giver of hope.

Barbara Drake

Driving 100

We went, in 1956, in Sarah's boyfriend's car
out on the new highway south of Coos Bay,
toward Millington, named for a mill,
and the Shinglehouse Slough,
where years later someone's father's ashes
would be scattered, his last wish.
We went in Sarah's boyfriend's car,
a black convertible,
and she, wishing to try on speed,
drove fast, fast, faster,
pushing the speedometer to sixty,
seventy, eighty, as we screamed
and laughed and held ourselves down
in the seats without seatbelts.
Our hair in the wind lashed us
like something breaking over a waterfall,
and afraid our young meat and bones
would be scattered,
we screamed at Sarah, slow down slow down,
Sarah, and then she did ninety
laughing, "He'll kill me if he ever finds out,
you guys, don't tell," and pushed the pedal
down and held it, as we went fast, and faster,
screaming and dying and laughing at Sarah,
until the needle stood at one hundred,
and Sarah relented, and we chided her then,
and began to breathe again,
at sixty, fifty, forty, did a U at twenty,

turned around at the cutoff to Coquille.
"I almost died," we all said.
"I'll never do that again."
And our flesh settled down to go on living
as we secretly thanked her, like a goddess,
for the terrible experience.

A Piece of Cake

Did you get a lunch?
my husband asked,
as I was about
to run out the door.
Oh no, I said, went back
and grabbed some cheese, threw
it between 2 pieces of bread.
Tossed it in a sack.

Wait, he said, I saved you
a piece of cake.
Half of that, I said.
I watched him cut the cake in half.
I hoped he would like the other half.
I watched him tear
a piece of wax paper, wrap
it carefully around the cake
making a nice package.
He put it and an orange in my sack.
His fingers were stained
from husking walnuts.
The cake had walnuts on it.
He had his red plaid jacket on
to walk me to the car.
Blue fog outside was lifting.

I said, if lonely spirits were here
they'd look at us and think
how good it is to be alive.
He said, are spirits lonely?
Don't they have any place to go?

Charles Goodrich

Vacuuming Spiders

I admire their geometrical patience,
the tidy way they wrap up leftovers,
their willingness to be the earth's
most diligent consumers of small bitternesses.

Sometimes at night I hear them
casting silk threads, clicking their spinnerets,
plucking their webs like blind Irish harpists.
I can almost taste the fruit of the fly
like sucking the pulp from a grape.

But when their webs on the ceiling
begin to converge, and the floor
glitters with shards of insect wings,
I drag out the vacuum
and poke its terrible snout under the sofa,
behind the radio—everywhere,

for this is the home of a human being
and I must act like one
or the whole picture goes haywire.

Rototiller

This winter
when my wife cut my hair
I swept the trimmings from the floor
and stashed them in a paper bag
along with a year's worth of finger- and toe-nail clippings
and little blood-spotted wads of toilet paper
from shaving nicks.

And this morning, under clouds
layered gray like a sowbug's carapace,
the rank grass lacquered
with the afterbirth of devas,
and the rented tractor idling by the fig,
I make my prayers on the ground
and sprinkle my dead cells here and there.

Now
till in the vetch, the rye grass and the crimson clover,
the daisy, dandelion, thistle and bindweed;
till in the blood meal and bone meal,
the finely dried gore of the abattoir;
till in the rock phosphate mined god-knows-where,
and the kelp meal with its potent minerals and fragrance of the sea;

till in the compost, the witch's cake
of layered maple leaves, donkey manure,
vegetable ends, eggshells, floor sweepings, coffee grounds,

till it in faster now
twenty-two hundred r.p.m.

the diesel roaring happily
it was made to burn
and stir this small pathetic superstitious gardener's
sluffed off body parts
into heavy clay loam
into fertile, but poorly drained, basaltic soil

till it in,
till in the clearcut Coast Range,
the channeled and dammed Willamette,
the poisoned farmland, the incarcerated schools,

till in the Kalapuyas, the brown bears and the blue camas,
till in the beaver-trappers, the beavers and turkey vultures,
till in the missionaries, the migrant workers and Wobblies,

till in H. L. Davis and Hazel Hall,
Walt Curtis and William Stafford—
what the hell! till in Hesiod's *Works and Days,*
Lao Tzu, *Walden,* and *Chilton's Toyota Pickup Truck Repair Manual,*

till it all in,
your mother's little skeleton, the ashes your father left,
your forty-odd, equivocal years,
till it in, till it in
for the new garden.

Donna Henderson

The Sanctuary

It was late when I walked up the gravel
road to the clear-cut hill. Loggers gone
for the day, feller-buncher machines all still,
their claws and blades cooling.
A low sun laid its thick light on the slope,
the light sieved through the last, lean stand.
Into those wrecked woods I walked,
straight to the center pile,
laid myself down on a log
and apologized for my species.

Oh, I apologized to those tears for my species
with tears, but not without greed:
I wanted a word in turn.
Of forgiveness, reassurance,
I don't know—I wanted a word.
Which didn't come.
And what was I thinking, wanting more?
The trees, after all, were dead.

The trees were dead; only the light was there.
Which I saw (as I stood between the machines
and their gruesome business, amid the piles and vines),
coated the whole sorry mess of us all,
without chastisement or preference.

Without chastisement or preference the light
left, and I walked back down that road
and up my own, home to a solitude I was
bereft of now, sullied as it was.
Woke the next day to watch, over again,

one fir after another lean to the left
and fall, keening and cracking (*Screamers*,
the Canadian painter Emily Carr had called them:
final splinters that shriek as the trunk is torn).
For so long—oh, *forever*—I had counted on the forest's
persistence there, its green and cool surround.
Not to escape the sufferings of the world:
from which to bear them.
Now the violence was taking the forest, too
while I stood on my cedar deck,
inconsolable, seeing unceasingly.

Inconsolable, seeing unceasingly
a word arrived through the wound—
                    This is what it is to bear witness,
I saw inside. As the woods get small
the heart had to grow larger. To become,
by its breaking, what those woods had been.
Spacious, the heart would have to become,
and huge. Enough to hold all the trees
and their absence, and every other thing.

First Ice

We wake up as the darkness begins
giving way, first to an indigo

glow like laundry bluing,
phosphorescent and implausibly dense.

Shades of trees appear, then trees,
then a dreamy, scintillant

stillness unfurls as light, as landscape
under a spell. A fat sleekness

blisters and thickens the porch; in the pasture
grass blades bow down in glass sleeves.

The woods are themselves and not
themselves in their subtle glister,

the way a truly glamorous woman,
my grandmother used to say (charm bracelets rustling),

conceals every seam and trace
of her artifice, leaving pure effect.

Inside, a chef on TV makes aspic
while we wait for the forecast.

*One strives for the clearest, thinnest
gel,* he is saying; *one wants to illuminate*

one's terrine, not to thicken it!

And as he spreads his glaze, I see the soul

rise from its loaf and lay its glossy
immaterial bliss across that surface of meat &

salt with its scallion *fleur-de-lis,*
making it marvelous.

As the world is, today—as it was
in the beginning, that last instant

water, matter, and light were one,
each distinct, not yet separate.

Poetry
(palindrome and calligramme)

A way   a way.
   whereby   whereby
     sounds   sounds
       make   make
         geese

Lee Hettema

Here Comes the Queen

It is surprising what you can learn listening to a baseball game
broadcast on the radio.
Admittedly the Mariners are not doing very good this year.
So the patter between pitches and between innings
must be that much more interesting, to keep the fans' attention.
Two longs, a short, and a long are blown as the train approaches
    every intersection.
That is Q in Morse Code. It implies "here comes the queen."
Only on the railroad does the Hogger have his hands on the
    controls of the Queen.

Larry Hobart

Word Shortage

My vocabulary is limited
It knows words but very few
If I knew the words of Webster
I'd write better poetry for you.

I'd expedite and conjugate
The lexicographer's word
I'd have them turning somersaults
You would take me for a nerd.

I'd postulate and capitulate
Across the empty page
I'd abbreviate and speculate
I would be a writing sage.

I'd deviate, devastate, and detonate
Our language's most common words
Just to add a little ginger
To give my words a surge.

If you need a dictionary
To decipher what I have said
Then this poem is not for you
Rather the egalitarian instead.

Karen Holmberg

The Inkling

I surfaced to the faintest *chink* of shades
against closed windows, then submerged

again as a waft of air cooled
my cheek; a blind ethereal

hand was lightly sweeping over everything
in my dark dream shop, opening a case

to finger the moonstone pendant on a chain,
to feel for the platinum band on a plaster hand

resting its brittle shield upon a hemisphere
of breast. Then you snapped on

the reading lamp and light vibrated
in the air, a resonance so keen and high

the tympani can't communicate it
to the mind. It bathed your hip in dry brilliance,

archaic and unkissable. Like something seen
always out the corner of the eye, the bat

sailed with an erratic yet humid and
elastic poise over and under the beams, till

in a plummet (a limp glove tumbling
story after story from a hotel room)

the black silk was drawn through the knot
of an invisible fist.

Cold Storage

A door quilted with riveted lead—at a turn
        of the brass wheel
a puff of cloud vapor
        glazes the eye, mellows to a curtain
            you can walk through.

A caged bulb picks out gritty bronze or maroon
        glossy between the slats
of bushel crates stacked
        ceiling high. And Papa sends a basket clicking
            down a conveyor lined

with twinkling wheels, nodding you to pick
        out what you want:
Roxbury Russet, Kendall,
        Colvis Spice. You want one
           of everything, already

training your palm to gauge an apple's
        density, know
skin from skin (tight-
        waxed, or a fine garnet paper scuffing
           the hand), to name the variety by

thumbing the breadth of the blossom end
        Nonesuch   Northern Spy
where stamens crumble crisp
        as cinders knocked from the bowl
           of a cherrywood pipe.

Ruth Hudgens

Yellow Rose

What is it about you,
Yellow Rose
that makes me swoon
that curls my knees
beneath your bloom?

Were you Rose Wine
I'd be dizzy
Were you Rose Pudding
I'd be full
Were you Rose Balm
I'd be healed

What is it about you,
Yellow Rose
that makes me swoon
that curls my knees
beneath your bloom?

You are Rose Wine
and I am dizzy
You are Rose Pudding
and I am full
You are Rose Balm
and I am healed

Black Leather and the T&R

The other night I had the most vivid craving for
time at the T&R Truck Stop
smoking cigarettes, drinking alcohol,
hanging out with tattooed men and women
from everywhere in the country and
beyond.
I'd think about nothing at all in particular but would laugh
aloud at the wonder and absurdness of it all
wearing my short black leather skirt.

There'd be talk of small places in Georgia and those
long times between loving arms,
crocodiles that eat dogs in Florida,
and the people who both damn and save this country
and those people
would be called names I can't repeat and I would
give 'em hell for their racist, pig-headed, pea-brained
notions and they'd call me a bleeding heart, a naïve
innocent. So be it.

Instead I stood at the T&R gas station
lit up a bummed generic cigarette
and marveled at how I can still wear
that short black leather skirt and
how I can still want to be on the road
after all I know now.

Henry Hughes

Wasp-Wasted

Wasp,
the new shot
bartender Ben dreamed up
before closing—
you'll feel a sting

like nothing.
My head bobbing up
some two-pointed ladder
toward that papery gray nest
and yellow cinched
droptail black hover
of wasp on wasp

that sent me down
a coward, flailing and unstung.
So I spend my life
grounded, thickening
beer-slung
by the chlorinated pool

under pruned oaks,
while lithe, stripling boys
climb our peeling towers
slaying everything

but the urge
to take my slender wife
stepping wet
and horneted
from the upstairs
shower.

Eating Tuna

They laughed at my case of tuna.
It's a fishing boat, you dumb fuck. But halibut's
slime and money. I like a soft pink breakaway—
mayo and a splash of vinegar
on toasted white. Creamy, salty,
fishy in all the right ways.

Eating my sandwich
on a long-liner, twenty miles
off the Oregon coast, I read
the can's "Fish Tales":

The blue sea star regenerates a new body
from a single severed arm. The arm looks
like a long tail with a tiny star at its base
and is commonly called a comet.

Sure, I wish for fish
and watch myself. Lose something in that winch,
it ain't growing back.

It used to be stars & stories,
providence & prayer for the old mariners.
Now we got GPS and sonar, commissions and quotas.
The skipper spots a comet, and we say, *Cool, a comet.*

Back home, crusty and shriveled,
it's a long, hot shower, then between the sheets
where the world rolls over. Misty moons

on Lisa's blue panties
as she climbs in after work, her arm reaching for the light
'cause she thinks I'm sleeping. Cloud kiss, caress,
and that dive under the sky
where the tight ripples says *sea, sea,*
everything's so good.

Marilyn Johnston

July Fourth

He can't let go of the image:
rocket and artillery rounds lighting up the sky
overhead, blasts reflecting off Thu Bon River;
the incessant rattling of earth, and at dawn,
the hunks of shrapnel that shredded his tent walls,
missing his body by inches.

He figured he'd survived this long,
and, *Hell,* wouldn't it be downright cruel
to take him now, after nineteen months
in 'Nam and just hours before
his discharge, a plane taking him
far away from Da Nang.

He says it didn't take long to become
a fatalist—to believe the only thing separating
those who lived and those who died was *luck*—
particularly during days on jungle patrol
in 120-degree heat.
Sweat rolling down like hate.

But God knows, he still can't shake it.

Each summer for the past thirty-two years,
he tells me that story as we sit on the grassy
Willamette River bank—then silently wait
for the first boom, the first blast,
the lights brightening up
the night sky.

The Day After the Guest Speaker Talks About Darfur

1.

Last night's photo
flashed by the
presenter
on the screen
stays with me:
Thin woman,
child hugging
her leg.
Dirt path,
burned hut.

2.

Early morning,
soft rain on the roof.
Your hand
rubbing my back.
I wake up
from warm sheets.
You've left a bowl
of cereal
for me
on the counter.

3.

An
accident
of
birth...
or
aren't
we
really
all
Darfur?

4.

I drive to work.
A shoe
lies
discarded
in the street,
and no one
knows where
where
to find you
anymore.

Stephen Landolt

Goddess

She likes roses and running water,
Aphrodite does, and also
Eucalyptus leaves.
I know her address, but she's not home.

Swan Dive

Bungee jumping off my dresser
Shoelaces knotted to my ankles and the drawer-pulls
Studying the floor below for fortunate gullies
Where I might get by with only a broken neck.

There's thwarted passion in these plunges:
Remember the look in the coyote's eyes
When the roadrunner enticed him over
Yet another animated 1000 foot cliff?
Something more than fear of despair there
As he scrabbled at the edge before falling.
And then the tiny ring of dust when he finally hit bottom:
What a meticulous observance of scale.

And so, gathering breath and spreading arms wide,
I plunge in the final swan dive
Confident of tasting the oak bouquet
Of the floor.

Patricia Ann Love

Winter's Eve

Look! Flicker and towhee and junco have come,
three kings bringing gifts with quickness and grace
on winter's eve when earth is nearly numb
with exhortations to buy beyond means, efface

the landscape, go be vaccinated, make war.
While moon's weak glow barely penetrates
consumptive haze that wraps earth like tar
from oil spills suffocating murres, egrets,

and cormorants alike, the royal birds feast
on seed, without avarice or wantonness,
to honor tree frogs and all creatures least
survivable, doomed by ways mindless.

They pray for nesting turtles in the path of trucks
and for music makers who would stay destruction.

T'ai Chi on the Beach

A man and a woman in tandem
ever so slowly lean weight
onto a forward foot and stretch
one arm in front as if
reaching for something ahead
then swivel with both arms raised
open-handed toward the sun
about to flatten against a fog bank
unrolled along the whole horizon
foretelling pale rapid nightfall.

How lovely if we could keep
the melting polar ice caps at bay this way
melding spirits with simple fluid movements.

How hopeful if we could save ourselves
and all living creatures by rhythmic gestures
our bodies completely synchronized
with the planet's pulsations
our enterprises in harmony
with each other's giftedness.

I doubt the woman and man
know I am here. I doubt they care
that though their way is not my way
it matters to me I see them.

They give all things I love
new significance: walnut meat ingeniously
protected inside its shell yet

quickly accessible when time is right
for a clever scrub jay to feast;
a friend's ashes scattered in the foothills
along with season's last rose petals;
first frost made tolerable by flannel sheets.

Kelley Morehouse

A Winter Poem

If love were as simple as warm
breath on a chilly day,
an ecstatic embrace in the air
both instinctively make.
But centuries of heavily
embroidered garb
wrap round
my ways of love,
till I can hardly move.

I'd shed them all
to plunge fresh pools;
imagination seep
beneath my thirsty
skin, infusion
and reception
of some equivalent:

sweet as orange blossoms
bursting, stars surging
through the body
overflowing from my lips,
little cries of joy.

Even in the midst of winter.

Paulann Petersen

A Little Perspective

Seen close enough,
tungsten atoms make
a starburst. Farthest galaxies,
a prick of light.

Tungsten traces lay inside
the tomato I ate this morning.
Its globe held in one hand,
I took it into me

bite by bite. Juice and seed
smeared my chin.
Love apple.
Small, red sun.

Our galaxy lies inside
a cosmos waiting
to swallow me whole—
night coming, fast.

Time-Travel

The last time I see the man
I was wife to for twenty years
(give or take a year/give, be taken)
he's fallen asleep while

I sleep, dreaming his face
slumped into the steering wheel
of the car he drives. His passenger—
what else?—I cry out, rile him

to open his eyes. My left hand
(ringed? I don't see) reaches over
to turn the wheel a little,
and we're safe. I rouse

before a blow of his anger
*what the hell? why didn't you
do something sooner?*
can travel the distance between us—

the righted car gone,
the road now a part of itself
that lay ahead, out of sight.
I walk it alone, awake.

Dan Raphael

The Cherry Tree at the Top of the Stairs

as if its spring in the lung, the angle of shadow
a blossom that cant be got out of
16 of me
in a chain-reaction crash
up the stairs
i want to go out the window
and through the hole at the top of the cherry tree
where all the wishes of photosynthesis put down roots
& a glut of suns returning for an encore
a hot magnesium date

a mystery time can't corrode
just costume
stewed in spring
dried when the suns on the rocks
rubbed into the genitals when preparation seems impossible
dancing to the strange light
as if the sky unzipped
i want accident, not order
as if repetition could lead to the exceptional
using everything but names

a sky so yellow one closes the shade
or jumps without falling
to claw my way into gluttony
letting nothing go to waste
terraforming my organs into microclimates rare & mundane
urban epiphytes;   highway clogged with marsupials
the rivers fluorescence is not a trick.

the heart knows too much jazz to stop growing fingers:
             a scalp full of reeds
       running in every direction and into myself
                   dancing on my own skull
                        belly stretched & dried,   thigh with all the stops o
     an organic chord the cherry blossoms run through all its changes
                 an aria scat upon the tongue
   arboretums of vital nutrients
             neath the rain red as cherries yet to come,
                 red as the breasts of stillborn birds
         where the sky is the earth exposing itself in all directions
           to jumpstart the ennui of hibernation
      to confuse the mower with more color than fashion can contain.

   i flow up from my roots, uncoil my shoulders and blow
             through the hole at the top of the cherry tree
             where all the wishes of photosynthesis
               go beyond and in-through the molecular time-signatures
                   to sprout a new jazz deafening in its silence,
                 hip irresistible spasms commingling in decomposition,
                 sprouting unthinkably green/alien/organic,
                        the sun the way to new worlds,
       so we go past the middle not stopping at solstice, at equilibrium,
             marrying the arctic to the solar,
                 the chakric void to electromagnetic profusion
   ripping time open to trees big as planets, planets small as cherrypits,
       people ripe as summer fruit fermenting in the sun of their mutual lo

Where you Been?

Ive been to the crow bar, the no bar, the low brow lounge,
someplace else, the office, the wunder bar, the bar none.

Ive eaten goat, stoat, twice rolled oats, mousse, elk, white tail
—just jumped out in front of the car.
ive had yak milk cheese, water buffalo salami, tofurkey, wham, meat
    whiz, slumgullion

Drank moonshine from my landlord, water from a bamboo sluice,
monongahela river water, a little bit of everything from my parents
    liquor cabinet,
drank moose piss, moose drool, cold cock, cloud nine
& what the gentleman on the floor is having

Ive swallowed enough chemicals
inhaled enough combustion
parlayed with kidnapped devas
let so many words explode inside me

If i never have another bite, another dram, another artificial brain
    elevation
i'll still be writing it down, making it up, boiling until tender,
forgetting that walls are solid, every utterance absorbed before it
    can get out,
cortex salad spinning, warm mist on the inside
remembering a density i'd itch and sneeze from

I split in five directions like a star without an exploding middle,
a space gravitys not allowed, not believed in:
the door opens around me, the floor folds up to chair me,
in my hand a glass, in my mouth many things

Lois Rosen

Satin Doll

Eggplants live for elegance
Mae Wests of the garden
schemers seeking adventure
sick of parsley, manure
the daily pettiness of radish.

Each July day more succulent
they ripen into skin tight
black satin sheets
nothing else to wear
every voluptuous curve
more visible over time.

Gloating in sunlight
their favorite music
slow Ella.

Bosomy, bold, beautiful
and don't they know it.

My Building, Singer Arms

Bessie Smith, Ethel Merman
their huge voices wow Manhattan
belt tunes so loud
they shake Yankee Stadium
bleachers, box seats, the outfield,
vibrate the whole Bronx,
all the way to Yonkers.
So what if they use a microphone
to entertain a borough,
let alone a whole city
the size of New York,
make music pour straight
like rain from the air?

Everyone here knows their style.
Look at how many minks
and sables they own,
their inky gowns, sequins
shimmering.
No measly man will dare
order a big-time star
to tie on an apron, scrub
his crummy floor,
bring him his meatloaf.

Nobody tells a Sophie Tucker
to go on a diet,
drink fewer egg creams,

cut down on the caramel.
One of these days, you're
gonna miss me, Honey,
she croons. Sorry, chump,
it's too late for a man
who can't appreciate
a woman who will not
keep her mouth shut.

Mark Sargent

To the Grave of Nikos Kazantzakis

A firm warm wind fans dawn Heraklion,
stilettoed party girls teeter home,
cleaning ladies wait for buses,
the morning catch iced and glistening.

Up Evans Boulevard toward Knossos
I turn at the great Venetian wall and ascend;
first sun flashes 'cross the city to the Cretan sea,
the sprinklers spring to life,
no matter,
who but poets visit at this hour?

The crude wooden cross sunk in concrete
is splintering, the crosspiece will soon give way;
in his script, scratched in a concrete slab,
the famous words declaiming
his lack of desire and fear,
the reward of freedom it brings.

But the world he spoke to
is bored, fat with its freedom,
puzzled by his passion
and hires others to do the fighting.

*

*"Return where you have failed,
leave where you have succeeded,"*
runs an old Cretan saying,
his last years spent in France
to return in a box.

Mount Yiouhtas to the south reveals
the face of the sleeping Zeus,
light glints off a speck of white
on the god's nose, a chapel, they say;
the church fears spirit, defends order,
grabs whatever land it can and refused
to bury this man, the earth upon this wall
unconsecrated by the priests of Crete.

*

With a stone to hold it, I leave a slim volume
of my verse, The Body Prays, a title he would like,
so full of prayer he was,
of spirit manifest in flesh,
of blood-thick reach for what cannot be had.

The time of *The Great Act* is over,
nothing rises above the tumult for long,
irony and nihilism have rendered us
incapable of believing that art can transform.

But without that faith, what can be made?

Those who come after, hear my prayer:
In the name of all poets,
for all keepers of the spirit,
as the thousands before have done in their turn,
I consecrate this earth
in recognition of his holy passage
upon this merciless terrain.

May poets in the 22nd century make pilgrimage
to this holy ground without despair,
hearts in their mouths,
to renew this prayer.

Virtual Garland

Okay,
I thought yesterday
was today, that
my few and meager obligations
were on the horizon still,
oh bone-idle swine that I am.

I take solace from Ms. Stein's dictum
that to be a genius requires
sitting around doing absolutely nothing
for inordinate amounts of time.

Well, no one's accusing me
of genius, but I've got the
doing bugger-all down cold,
so who knows,
maybe that laurel wreath
is somewhere up ahead?

I hope there's not a ceremony
where you have to show up
to receive your accolades,
that sounds a bit much and surely
in this era a courier is in order,
or something cyber-sent,
mere electronic suggestion
of esteem from somewhere
out there.   Yes,
that would do nicely.

Penelope Scambly Schott

In this Time of War,

I've rummaged too long in my dresser drawers sniffing
at dead sachets. Even the rose petals are scraps

of paper with no names written down. So how
must I dress myself to walk about upon

this reddened earth? Today I will wear my snazzy
new panties of snake skin, those cool translucent scales

that slither in only one direction, up.
Never to droop or gather about my ankles.

I once knew a woman who lived through the London Blitz,
and her knickers were stitched from German parachute silk—

all the elastic had gone to the army, only
a safety pin to hold her homemade panties

up; she stood on the platform at Waterloo Station
where a long troop train chugged in with the wounded,

and just as her right hand ascended to her forehead
in quick salute, her slippery silk panties descended

and puddled over her sensible shoes, and she stepped
right out of them and kept on walking

leaving all that tender and airworthy silk
under the crooked and shell-shocked wheels

of the gurneys, many,
so many gurneys.

My Father's Employment

Such a demanding job: another ordinary Wednesday
and you're still dead.

This weekend, you'll be dead too. Don't you ever get
a day off?

I am shaking the dry coins of the Chinese money plant.
Look,

you can see through each disk into the bright kingdom
of precious objects

that don't exist. I would spend every leaf in my garden
to cover your wages

for half an hour so you might knock off and sit with me
here in the striped shade

of stripped branches and we might sip our tea in tall
glasses of air.

Suppose I go put the kettle on. A white wicker table
and a painted chair

wait under the big maple. Now I am pouring the water
over your ashes.

Let us drink tea together after they steep.

When You Phoned Home from California
to Tell Me It Had Started

A brilliant globule of blood
rolled out over the surface of the desert
up and down the Continental Divide
through the singing prairies
parting the Mississippi
leaping the Delaware Water Gap
until it spilled into this tall red kitchen
in Rocky Hill, New Jersey
where it skittered across the linoleum
and cracked into hundreds of little faceted jewels.

I will not diminish this day with labeling
I will not say foolishly
now you are a woman
I will never tell you
don't talk to strangers

because we are each of us strangers
one to another
mysterious in our bodies,
the connections between us
ascending like separate stone wells
from the same dark water
under the earth

But tonight you delight me like a lover
so that my thigh muscles twitch
and the nipples of my breasts

rise and remember
your small mouth

until I am laughing to the marrow of my bones
and I want to shout
Bless you, my daughter, bless you, bless you;
I have created the world in thirteen years
and it is good.

Peter Sears

The Foam Machine

What if you were a fire burning out a house?
You can't last forever, you know it, but for now
you're better than all the shouts, sirens, and water
they can throw at you.
Heck, they can line up the engines
and try to drown you in a broadside, but they can't touch
your lick and laugh.
You steam the water into a skin
and work yourself up for a higher leap.
Who knows, you might reach a star
and blaze away happy
—when up skids another firetruck
and two firemen lift off a big metal box with a hose
the size of a sewer pipe.
You're going to broil it and spit out the metal pieces.
Oh how you love the smell of burning rubber!
Go ahead, you guys, jam that box on the front door
like a toilet plunger.
You're all over it,
but it won't burn. The hose foams,
the front room foams. It eats your air. You flash,
stagger, rush for the walls. A lather coating
cuts you off. You lick away
to another room. You're not up
to making a run for it,
and if you try to fatten up, it will find you, you know it.
So it's huddle in a corner.
Foam feels you out and feeds.

A Full Day of Shining

The hay field, just cut, is bright from a full day of shining.
I pull my cap down for easier squinting.

The sun's glow spreads along the horizon like a sauce.
Can the sunset brighten even more?

The next few minutes will tell.
I take a deep breath and adjust the brim of my cap.

Lose a Few

I come out of the nursery with my cactus,
and this lovely woman, walking by, starts talking
about my cactus.
She knows more about it than I do.
I ask her if she would like to have a lemonade.
Yes she would
and she would like to go to a place nearby she knows.

At the restaurant, we sit outside
and watch people walk by on the boulevard.
I'm thinking wouldn't it be great if my friends
drive by and see me with her.
The waiter winks at her.
I am feeling so good I wink at the waiter.
She and I have that easy talk you want to have
with a lovely stranger on a dazzling day in the city.
So when she has to be going,
I ask her could I call her and would she
give me her phone number? She does,
on a coaster. We stand up, shake hands, and say goodbye.
I have to hold on tight not to start dancing around.

I wait a whole day to call. Nerves.
When I phone, a gruff voice answers "City Morgue."
Before I understand that I've been had,
I ask for her. The gruff voice laughs.
I understand, I'm embarrassed.
When I see her again, and I do see her on the boulevard,
about the same place we first met,
I want to hide. She tricked me,
but if I can't take it, I might as well just go to the movies.
I wave hello and she,
hesitating at first, waves back.

Ginger Fennimore Shull

Communion

I knew where to get water
and it wasn't at the kitchen sink.
I didn't carry a canteen either.
I collected it in the cup of my hand,
on the lap of my tongue
from the spring
beneath the ancient fir
where the water ran
from immemorial seepage
and cooled unknown,
unnamed peoples
who were revived in my partaking.

Ponderosa Pine

An easy target, we kids raced toward the pine tree
 needing to win the best mount for swinging.
"Go for the limb with the dusty well under it!"
I would say, "It's the greatest."
There, with hydraulic legs, we met and exceeded
the speed and pulse of swaying branches above us
which were moved only by the wind.

Opening frenzy of the first ride shifted into
a slower gait matching the breathing of the limbs
eighty feet above. Then, I could listen
(if I were quiet) to the centuries old pine
exhaling mysteries of others who had touched it,
even planted it on this route
of the north-south Klamath Indian trail.

The swoosh of swift feet carrying obsidian,
beads, slaves, seeds, animals, food
shuffled in the needles, cones, boughs,
but only for a moment or two
before my young senses lost it
and the "yippees" of high-riding siblings
erased the sacred glimpse.

It was right to pay homage.

Michael Smith

A Studio

                              shut the door
then I'm out in my chicken house
imagining a place
                              all mine
not part of us love partnership
if I were thinking what would I be
                              thinking about
I'm there something arises chocolate
smooths the waning afternoon after
                              siesta tasks
accomplished together an outing
                              in disguise
I go to the chicken house write
by natural light look inward ride
                              music
listen to the flowing creek
watch days seasons pass learn
                              stillness
compassion equanimity exercise art
be an artist in my studio make
                              expression

Civic Duties

there now the weekend gone not regretted
civic duties private pleasures sunshine rain
whether accomplishing anything matters
wheels roll spin juices flow nothing stays
home knitting thinking guillotine passages
cataracts tintinnitus stews ejaculations
cool fingers yellow red tulips deer fence
box office attention festival publicity due
link my pages wireless virtual magic spell

Joseph A. Soldati

The Bikers at Starbuck's

They look more like Willie Nelsons than Che Guevaras.
Yet their carefully unkempt beards and combed pony tails
are as authentic as the earrings, head scarves, dark glasses, and boots.
Most have stripped off their leather jackets
to reveal arms gilt black and blue with tattoos.
But drinking double-shot-skinny-decaf-mocha lattes?
When summer comes will they switch to Frappuccinos®,
lick the frosted foam from straws, and sigh, yuppily, in the sun?

A genuine Hell's Angel wouldn't even take off his helmet,
would order a cup of unground Guatemala, chew the beans
and spit the bitter leavings on the sidewalk—
all the time keeping one hand in the rear pocket of his mama's jeans,
while his huge hog, aslant and sputtering on the same sidewalk,
threatens passersby like a ravenous beast.

Starbuck's Sunday Bikers align their bikes
like icons on display, facing outward from the curb.
We thrill at the chrome glistening brighter than scalpels,
at the scarlets, blues, greens, yellows, and purples
more radiant than the tiles on a Thai temple:
Machine as art *and* religion,
and we suspect the Bikers have stayed up all night
cleaning and polishing every part and pipe for our adoration.

Still, those shining Suzukis, Yamahas, Harleys
entice us to pleasures beyond those complacencies of the peignoir
and the yawning stretch that connects a Sunday morning with its
     afternoon.
When the Bikers start their engines all roar and freedom—

a sound that softens men and hardens women—
then file up the avenue like a bright segmented dragon
breathing fire and defiance, we long to ride with them,
free from a Sunday of whatever responsibilities
got us no closer to God than we were last night,
into a paradise of metallic blue skies
with clouds the color of steamed cream atop a cappuccino.

Evening

Evening, with three syllables, *e·ven·ing*—
a slow-saying word the mouth hesitates
to let go—the evening of twilight
smoothing out the dents and spikes of day,
soothing the way a hand stroking your face
erases the creases of question and care.
Think of a river evening below the cataracts
or embanked below the wind's whirl;
of coals glowing without a flame;
of birds that fly without dip or swerve,
as if they'd found a groove in the sky.
Think of bread, unleavened,
that will not rise to insistent heat,
of a lake iced beneath a snow, the long
evening of a sandy shore counterpoised
against the sea. Think of how your breathing
softens after love, the evening of your body
dissolving into air.

Clemens Starck

Hitchhiking

I was standing by the side of the road
somewhere in Idaho,
thumbing a ride. I was headed back east.
From the map I could see that the shortest way
lay through Wyoming.

Hitchhiking was my magic carpet, but it required
perseverance—and luck.
What to do next? I wondered, while pondering
schemes that involved Argentina
or Iceland,
and a system for playing the horses...

Traffic was sparse, and no car stopped.
So after four hours I quit, walked back across town
and started thumbing again—
south this time, toward Utah.

A Few Words About Hope—and Baseball

Still one more month of hope
for Red Sox fans, as the Sox head back to Boston,
trailing the Yankees
by 3½ games.

Hope is also
the name of a town in B.C.
where I rendezvoused once with my wife and kids
while scouting the interior,
looking around for a place to spend
the rest of our lives.

According to Paul
in one of his letters to the Corinthians, hope
"abideth."
More than that, he doesn't say.

By definition, loss of hope is desperation or despair.

In any case, I'm sitting here at the kitchen table
reading the sports section—
checking the standings, studying
the box scores.

The Benefit of Smoking

"Smoking can pay off," says Jerry,
lighting another cigarette and telling how
in 1945, while serving aboard a destroyer in the Pacific,
he stepped out on deck once
for a smoke.

Seconds later, a shell
ripped through the bulkhead,
killing his buddies instantly, and sending him sprawling
across the deck,
shell-shocked but otherwise unharmed.

"So, you see, I wouldn't be here
if I didn't smoke," says Jerry, puffing away, still
bucking the odds at 83.

Nicole Taylor

I am not

I am not
the middle-aged guys
sitting in this coffee shop
playing chess.
I am
playing games with words.
I am not
the lady flipping off
the bus driver
reminding her of rules.
I am
the lady ignoring her
and putting my feet up
on a nearby seat.
I am not
the older guy reading
a Robin Cook mystery.
I am
reading ZYZZYVA,
the last word for West Coast
writers and artists.
I am
not the young guy
sitting across from me
talking about his addictions.
I am
the lady sitting
writing,
seeing a poem.

Jeremy Trabue

The Key Thing One Loves About Tomatoes in the Garden

is the smell, not a red smell—it's green—some kinda hairy green—
little fibery green stems & thick munchy leaves—pointy—that's
what's lost in the grocery store and—almost gone going quick even
in the kitchen on the windowsill pretty much gone by the fruit stand
really—there's just a little red smell still (the taste is red) but that
fresh tomato smell, that tomato in the garden smell—that's green—
that's green—it's a chlorophylly smell all plant magic green—it's the
exact shade of green that the stem is when you break it too high
picking the fruit and there's a rich darker wetter green inside that
pale hairy green—that fresh tomato smell is that glistening darker
vivid plant magic green inside the broken stem and fading as it
dries—you could sit inside that tomato patch and smell that smell all
day till you were green yourself and almost full and sick of it—that's
that fresh green green tomato smell—it's not red—it's green, it's in
the garden, it's fading as it dries—

Laura D. Weeks

Boltzmon's Last Set

For Alex, and for the beautiful dancer right below the keyboard

It all happened way back,
Back when Boltzmon
Was frontman
For the Sisterhood of the Travelling Pants.

He'd slip out between sets
Grab a cute little number in the crowd,
Slide behind the counter
Still be-boppin', a-chatterin'

—Wired, I tell you!—
Head still snappin',
Fingers still walkin' the moons
Between the changes.

Us? We chugged our beer, quiet-like,
But Boltzmon, he never touched nothin'.
(Never needed it, neither!)
"Not while I'm workin', boys!"

Then he'd shimmy on up to the stage.
Firecracker eyes, smile so wide
You could number the stars.
"You're a beautiful crowd!"

Christ, that boy could charm!
His words slid glissando
Over their foreheads.
"You want more music?"

"Yeah-ah-ah!" Then the drums start talkin':
Kunga and bongo,
Djembe and tom-tom
Flim-flam-a-diddle and didgeridoo

'Til your scalp flips open
Your brains take a hike,
But your feet stay planted
On account of the vibes,

Those oh-so-low vibes
Crawlin' up your leg.
Boltzmon, Boltzmon,
Nobody seed the subtle knife comin'.
Nobody knowed
It was the summer to die.

Tomorrow's Forecast

A cold spleen moves over the deeps
Trailing a scarf of fog
Over the salt flats of my mind.
Pressure, as of a brooding storm,
Batters my eardrums, and I know
Sure as you might say,
"Looks like rain,"
Or, "Feels like thunder!"
Tomorrow I will writhe,
The booming surf inside my head, the vertigo
Dogging my uncertain steps.

Outside my head
It's uncommonly quiet.
I can no longer tell
One sound from another:
A barking dog? Bleating brass?
A handsaw's hollow rasp?—It's all one.
What sound comes,
Threading an ever smaller needle,
Scars my hearing—a thin red streak of sound.
Tomorrow, I'll flounder in the swell;
Tonight I ride

The eye of the storm.

Christopher Michael Wicks

Sonnet 16

All night last night I heard the ocean roaring,
The ocean, grey and blue and black and deep.
I would that I my soul in her could steep,
With gulls and eagles over my head soaring.
Some say she is the mother of all living.
Then is it for her children she is crying?
Thinks she on me, who for lost love am dying?
The sea neither condemns nor is forgiving.
It seems to me at times she's almost singing,
A savage song, exultant and eternal,
Of depths and heights, the mundane and supernal;
She fills our ears with shout and song and ringing.
I fret and stew o'er how and why and where:
She roars and sings and shouts. She doesn't care.

Sonnet 33

My love is pure, my love is transcendental,
My love has wings for feet and stars for eyes;
Its mother's the earth; its father is the skies.
My love is physical, my love is mental,
My love's progress is sure and incremental;
My love is foolish, and my love is wise;
There's nothing in you my love can't surmise;
My love is passionate; my love is gentle.
Perhaps you wonder whose my love may be,
This beneficiary of my heart,
And whether my beloved's kind or true—
You silly thing! If you had eyes to see,
You wouldn't need arcane divining art—
It's obvious that my beloved is you!

Matt Yurdana

Checkup for the Tattooed Man

She holds the stethoscope
near the mouth of a small purple carp

and a faint and muffled murmuring
rises between his third and fourth rib,
spine-deep, so that the sycamores, caged parrots,
and a sun whose rays curl loosely
around his navel, all seem a part of the water
the carp is swimming through.

And again, much louder, under daffodils
at sunrise, beneath a crane's silhouette,
below his left nipple.

There's no way to diagnose
this landscape which is his body,
nothing to prescribe that would make sense
of all she's heard,

but she goes on listening
to the moon with bronchitis, a butterfly
holding hypertension
in its flamboyant wings, until she lifts her hand
and the world goes quiet.

And when she settles again
on his sternum, she's in a forest
where moss is bright green on the north face
of lodgepole pines,

where a lake is a bottomless blue
at the base of steep granite cliffs,
and a red rowboat sits oarless, in last light,
its bow nosing the gravel shore.

When she pushes off
it feels as though the boat is gliding,
her momentum like a magnet
drawn to the center of the lake,

and what was once shoreline is now a thin arc
where trees have fallen into place,
hiding everything behind a beautiful green
that floats over this field of blue,

but even out here she can't ignore
that the water is beating.

The Problem with Listening

At a time like this, he's simply helpless, his ears
like two little wells the world wishes in,

brimming with the first ingredients for Cajun tapenade,
three reasons to never buy a Ford, a cough and a sigh,
and somewhere near the restrooms the headlong sincerity
of a father explaining escrow to his son;

all this, while his girlfriend deliberates, a finger sculpting
the foam of her cappuccino, perfectly content to be
the only one in this café he can't hear.

If he's lucky, she thinks that he, too, is poised
on the edge of discussion,

but a man is unhappy with his washing machine
while one woman convinces another that a new haircut
might accentuate her cheekbones;

baseball scores, a back-handed compliment,
the polite but growing impatience with the new cashier,
and some kind of fight three tables over, every third word
an island above the whispering,

and above it all, Billie Holiday playing devil's advocate
in that sleepy, nonchalant way that reminds him
of his mother's humming when he was a boy,
Saturday mornings, summertime, the smell of pancakes:

my life a hell you're making
you know I'm yours just for the taking,

and he nods, studies the tabletop, strokes his chin
because he realizes that she's spoken and he's missed it,
her eyes saying ten, maybe fifteen seconds
before this silence lasts days, maybe a week,

leaving him no choice but to bet it all on what he thinks
is most probable, most dangerous; he smiles,
looks her in the eye, then says *yes.*

JUDITH BARRINGTON'S "Walking North" and "Harvest" are from *Horses and the Human Soul* (Storyline Press, 2004).

ELEANOR BERRY'S "Like Anenomes from the Blood of Adonis" was published in *Nimrod*; "Where Gravity Has Brought Them" in *Windfall.*

KAREN BRAUCHER'S "Jellyfish" and "Instructions" are from *Aqua Curves* (NFSPS Press, 2005).

VIRGINIA CORRIE-COZART'S "Friday Night Jam" first appeared in *Karamu;* "From the Annals of Ants" first appeared in *Prairie Star.*

MADELINE DEFREES'S "Climbing the Sky Bridge stair on my way to Suzzalo Library" was first published in *Spirituality & Health* and reprinted in *Montana Women Poets: A Geography of the Heart* (Farcountry Press, 2006); "The Poetry of Swans" and "The Spider in Brewer's Dictionary," first published in *The Southern Review*, are in her book *Spectral Waves* (Copper Canyon Press, 2006).

BARBARA DRAKE'S "Driving 100" appeared in *Left Bank* magazine; "A Piece of Cake" is from her chapbook *Small Favors* (Traprock Press).

CHARLES GOODRICH'S "Vacuuming Spiders" and "Rototiller" are from *Insects of South Corvallis* (Cloudbank Books, 2004).

DONNA HENDERSON'S "First Ice" appeared in *A Fine Madness.*

MARILYN JOHNSTON'S "July Fourth" is from her book *Red Dust Rising* (The Habit of Rainy Nights Press, 2004).

LOIS ROSEN'S "My Building, Singer Arms" appeared in the *2005 Oregon State Poetry Association Prizewinners' Anthology;* "Satin Doll" appeared in *Hubbub.*

MICHAEL SMITH'S "Civic Duties" appears at http://michaeltownsend smith.blogspot.com.

JOSEPH A. SOLDATI'S "Evening" first appeared in *Solo;* "The Bikers at Starbuck's" and "Evening" are in his chapbook *Apocalypse Clam* (Finishing Line Press, 2006).

LAURA D. WEEKS'S "Boltzmon's Last Set" and "Tomorrow's Forecast" appear in her chapbook *Deaf Man Talking.*

MATT YURDANA'S "Checkup for the Tattooed Man" and "The Problem with Listening" are from *Public Gestures* (University of Tampa Press, 2005).